Max and Elle's

Adventures with Electricity

By: Duncan Watt

say hi to
Max

and also to
Elle

Max and Elle's

Adventure with Electricity

By: Duncan Watt

Electricity is everywhere
it is part of nature.

You cannot **see it**,
or smell it,
or even taste it.

We use it in our **houses** and in our cities. Electricity can be used for almost anything!

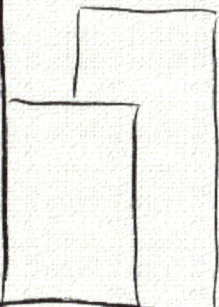

What is Electricity? It is the flow of tiny particles knowns as electrons and protons that move from place to place. The first people to talk about electricity were the **Egyptians** around **2750 BC** when they received shocks from eels in the Nile River.

Max and Elle
are best **friends**.

They love **nature**
and having many adventures.

One day Elle told Max,
"A storm is coming, and a kite is in the air."
And excited, Max answered,
"Let's go see and make it our **adventure!**"

How do we represent Electricity? Because it cannot be seen, scientists have represented electricity in many ways. It was in 1876 that **James Maxwell** showed it to us using mathematical formulas known as Maxwell's Equations (Max & Elle).

Suddenly thunder appeared,
and lightning struck.
Then **sparks** came down
towards a key in a jar.

With a glowing key in his hand,
Mr. Franklin was smiling happily.
Then he told Max and Elle,
"Come and see, electricity is **moving!**"

How does electricity move? Electricity moves through metal cables and wires like water through a hose. In 1752 **Benjamin Franklin** demonstrated this with his kite and key experiment, but do not do it because it is very dangerous.

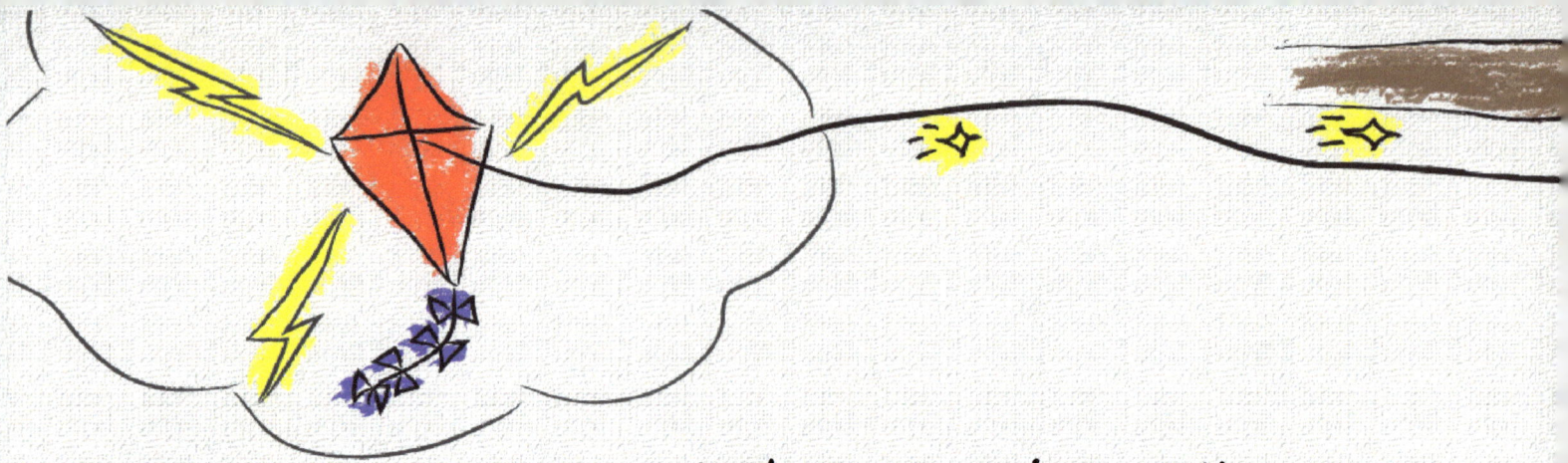

"Oh, I am quite wet",
Mr. Franklin said.
"Let's go to Mr. Edison's house
and find **light and comfort** instead".

When entering the house,
they saw a room all lit up.
"It's because of my **light bulbs**",
from a seat **Mr. Edison** pointed up.

How does a light bulb work? When electricity passes through some materials, these can produce light we call photons. In 1879 **Thomas Edison** produced the first commercial electric light bulb, giving us light and comfort until today.

When they left Mr. Edison's house,
the storm had stopped
but light bulbs were still shining.
"How can they **still be on**?"
Elle and Max were wondering.

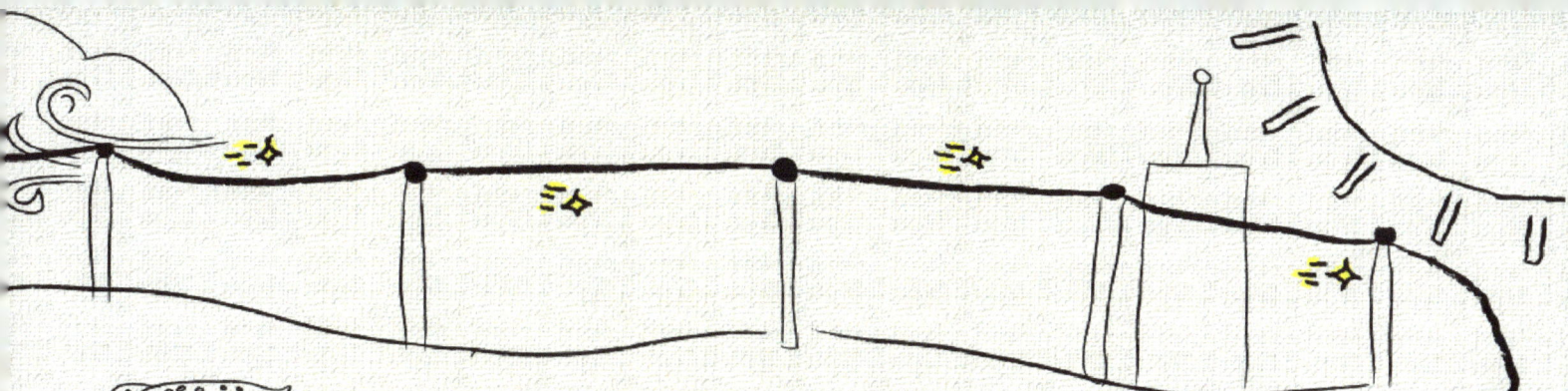

"Please come and visit my farm",
Mr. Volta said out loud.
"With the **batteries** I make,
we can have electricity all day long".

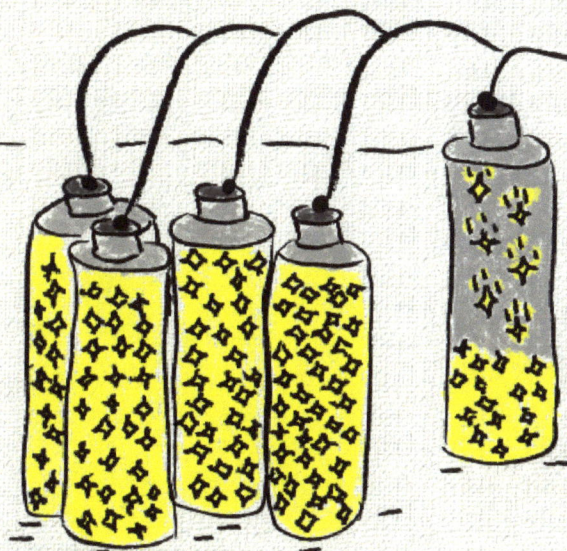

Can Electricity be stored? By itself, electricity cannot be stored like food or water. It must be transformed to another type of energy. In 1800 Alessandro Volta created the first battery called the "Voltaic Pile" storing electricity as chemical energy.

After leaving Mr. Volta's Farm,
Max and Elle were feeling quite **tired**.
Then a strange car stopped
with a motor in its tires.

"My car uses an **electric motor**", a happy **Mr. Faraday** told them. "If you need to go somewhere, I can take you there."

How do Electric Motors work? These motors are built with coils and magnets, and when electricity flows, they turn helping us to move many things. In **1821 Michael Faraday** made the first electric motor and in **1855** Anyos Jedlik presented the first electric car.

"Our parents don't know about this adventure!",
Once left by Mr. Faraday, both exclaimed.
But then they saw a couple **talking** into a box
and their curiosity kicked in.

"Use this **telephone** and call your parents",
Mr. and Mrs. Bell invited.
"Thank you, now they will know where we are",
Max & Elle happily replied.

RING RING!

BLA BLA

How can we talk using Telephones? This is because sounds can be transformed into electricity so they can travel long distances and then convert again to sound on the other side. In **1876 Alexander Bell** built the first telephone and now we can talk with anyone around the world.

17

While thanking Mr. and Mrs. Bell,
Max and Elle started hearing **music**.
But no band was playing
and nobody was singing.

"Please come to my party and dance if you please. The music is coming from my **radio**", **Mr. Marconi** said merrily.

How do Radios work? Electromagnetic waves are a type of electric energy that travels through space. Radios work by capturing these waves with antennas and converting them to sounds and information. In 1897 **Guglielmo Marconi** built the first radio using Nicola Tesla's wireless communications principles from 1893.

Max and Elle were feeling a bit hungry
after dancing with Mr. Marconi.
Then from a kitchen close by
the smell of delicious **food** came to them.

"Please come and eat with me", **Mr. Spencer** invited. "It comes from my **microwave oven**, and it's quite yummy indeed."

How do Microwave Ovens cook? By using specific electromagnetic waves, they cook food by heating the water inside them. In **1947 Percy Spencer** discovered this when candy melted in his pants while working on antennas, and his first microwave meal was popcorn.

FLOUR   SUGA   SALT   PEP

MICROWAVE

1200

Elle and Max were quite satisfied
after their meal with Mr. Spencer.
Then from the room next door
they saw a **movie** playing for real.

From his seat **Mr. Baird** said,
"Come here and accompany me.
Let us watch a movie in my **television**
while both of you rest your feet."

How do Televisions work? Televisions have screens with tiny light bulbs and when they receive electric signals an image is produced for us to see. In **1925 John Baird** built the first television and broadcasted to it a puppet called Stooky Bill.

Leaving Mr. Baird after the movie ended,
both noticed their stuff was **big and heavy**.
Then Max and Elle asked each other,
"How can we make them easier to carry?"

Laboratory

"Worry no more."
An excited **Mr. Bardeem** told them.
"With **transistors** we shrink anything,
making them easier to handle".

↑ Transistor ↖

←In   Out→

ON
OFF

What does a Transistor do? They allow equipment to use very little electricity, and by that they can be much smaller and transportable. In 1947 **John Bardeem** and a great team invented this component making our lives much easier now.

"We forgot about **homework**!",
Elle exclaimed while leaving Mr. Bardeem.
"What can we do?",
very worried Max said.

$1 + 1 = ?$

$2 + 2 = ?$

$3 + 3 = ?$

$4 + 4 = ?$

"My friends, please come on in",
from the classroom **Mrs. Hopper** said.
"Use my **computer** for your homework,
please go ahead."

How does a Computer work? They work with programs called "Software" that help us to do math, writing, listen to music and even watch movies. In 1944 *Grace Hopper* wrote the first software program for an electronic computer transforming in many ways how we do things today.

While thanking Mrs. Hopper for her help,
Max and Elle remembered
that today was their friend's birthday.
"How can we **greet him**?",
both of them wondered.

"Please do not worry",
calmly **Mrs. Lamarr** told them.
"Connect yourselves through my **WiFi Modem**
and use the Internet to talk to him."

What is WiFi Modem? It is a type of radio that allows electronic equipment to speak with each other transmitting information we call "Bits" without the use of cables through a world wide network we call the Internet. **Hedy Lamarr** in the **1940's** developed this technology and she was an actress too!

While celebrating with Mrs. Lamarr,
a telephone with an antenna was ringing.
They picked it up and answered,
"Hello, who is **calling?**"

BLA

BLA

"It is me **Mrs. Jackson**,
from my **mobile phone** you see.
There is a lovely day outside,
would you like to play with me?"

How do mobile phones talk to each other? They use many antennas inside cities and in fields. With them we can talk to anybody and from anywhere. In the **1970's Shirley Jackson** has invented several technologies even Caller ID which we use in mobile phones today.

After playing outside
Elle and Max came back **home**.

They changed the **light bulbs**
then charged some **batteries**,

and once all chores were finished
they made **microwave** popcorn.

Then heard music in the **radio** and watched some **television**.

INTERNET

After that, they chatted using **computers** and the **Internet**.

BLA BLA

They also used **mobile phones** and spoke to many friends all around the world.

33

Sometimes, friends
using computers and telephones,
would make fun of them.
Making Max and Elle
get **quite mad**.

Sometimes, Elle and Max
wanted to talk to a friend.
But they couldn't
answer their calls,
making both feel **really sad**.

But at the end of the day,
both felt something was **wrong**.

Max and Elle were feeling all alone,
forgetting about their adventures
and what they had learned all along.

Suddenly electricity stopped
and everything went **dark.**
"What should we do?",
Max and Elle told each other in awe.

Then they remembered
while looking at each other,
"Outside is full of **nature,**
let's go out and seek new **adventures!**"

The End

37

Notes for parents and adults:

This book tries to represent a journey through the history of electricity and electromagnetism using simplified concepts and inventions we are using until today.

Please always remember that electricity is very dangerous and touching it can be harmful for you and to children. Some drawings show activities and experiments, but these should always be done with the supervision of an expert in electricity.

Also, this book tries to send a message to both adults and children about how we use and how dependent on technology we are. There is so much to see in nature, but we tend to forget about it.

About the author:

Since I was a kid electricity has always marveled me. It feels like magic, making many things possible out of thin air.

I see scientists and inventors that made these discoveries as great magicians being able to answer and build these marvels that we use until today.

I want to thank Lucilia, my parents, brothers and sisters that inspired me to continue creating.

References for Inventions/Discoveries (Back Cover Page):

1. Differential Form Maxwell's Equations, Author: YassineMrabet
2. Franklin's Lightning Experiment – June 1752, Author: Currier & Ives
3. Ampule Originale de Thomas Edison – 1880, Musée des Letres et Manuscrits Paris, Author: Tieum512
4. Alessandro Volta's Voltaic Pile – 1800, Tempo Voltiano – Como Italy, Author: GuidoB
5. Faraday Electric Motor Diagram – 1821, Quarterly Journal of Science Vol. X11 – 1822
6. Pre-dial telephone – 1920, Patticheom Museum Limassol, Author: Catlemur
7. Marconi Type 3 Radio Receiver – 1920, Government License Examinations p.68, Author Elmer Eustice Bucher
8. Raytheon Microwave Oven on the NS Savannah, Baltimore Maryland – May 2012, Author: Acroterion
9. 1925 Television Transmission at London Dept. Store Selfridges, Popular Radio Magazine, Author: Orrin Dunlap Jr.
10. Replica of first transistor for 50th Anniversary of the invention – 1997, Author: Federal Employee
11. Atanasoff-Berry Computer at Iowa State University – 2006, Author: Manop
12. 1962 Bell 103 Analogue Modem, Author: Rebekah Magill
13. 1984 Motorola Dynatac 8000 with British Telecom Badge and Red LED Display – 2008, Author Redrum0486

References for Inventors/Scientists (page is indicated)

1. Page 7: Photograph of Young James Clerk Maxwell, Author: Unknown
2. Page 9: Portrait of Benjamin Franklin – 1778, Author: John Duplessis
3. Page 11: Portrait of Thomas Edison – Photographic Print, Circa 1922, Author: Louis Badrach – Badrach Studios New York
4. Page 13: Portrait of Alessandro Guisseppe Antonio Anastasio Volta, Author: Unknown
5. Page 15: Image of Michael Faraday holding a magnet – 1860, Author: Moll & Polybank
6. Page 17: Portrait of Alexander Graham Bell – between 1914 – 1919, Author: Moffet Studios
7. Page 19: Portrait of Gugliemo Marconi – 1908, Author Pach Brothers
8. Page 21: Photograph of Percy LeBaron Spencer, Author: Unknown
9. Page 23: Photograph of John Logie Baird – 1917, Author: Unknown
10. Page 25: Photograph of (from left) John Bardeem, William Shockley and Walter Brattain – 1948, Author: Jack St.
11. Page 27: Photograph of Grace Hopper in her Office – 1978, Author: Lynn Gilbert
12. Page 29: Hedy Lamarr Publicity Photo – 1944, Author: Unknown
13. Page 31: Photograph of Shirley Jackson in Annual Meeting – 2010, Author: Qilai Shen

www.ingramcontent.com/pod-product-compliance
Lightning Source LLC
Chambersburg PA
CBHW042116040426

42449CB00002B/63